THE BROAD
ART AND ARCHITECTURE

THE BROAD
ART AND ARCHITECTURE

THE BROAD   DelMonico Books • Prestel   MUNICH, LONDON, NEW YORK

Published in 2015 by The Broad and DelMonico Books, an imprint of Prestel
Publishing

The Broad
221 South Grand Avenue
Los Angeles, CA 90012
www.thebroad.org

Prestel, a member of Verlagsgruppe Random House GmbH

Prestel Verlag
Neumarkter Strasse 28
81673 Munich
Tel.: +49 89 4136 0
Fax: +49 89 4136 23 35

Prestel Publishing Ltd.
14-17 Wells Street
London WC1T 3PD
Tel.: +44 20 7323 5004
Fax: +44 20 7323 0271

Prestel Publishing
900 Broadway, Suite 603
New York, NY 10003
Tel.: +1 212 995 2720
Fax: +1 212 995 2733
E-mail: sales@prestel-usa.com
www.prestel.com

Editor in Chief: Joanne Heyler
Managing Editor: Ed Schad
Assistant Editor: Chelsea Beck
Designer: Makiko Katoh
Copy Editor: Megan Carey
Production: Luke Chase and Karen Farquhar
Printed and bound in China

Back cover: Jeff Koons, *Rabbit*, 1986 (page 56)

Pages 2–3: Installation in The Broad's third floor galleries including works
by Sherrie Levine, Robert Therrien, and Barbara Kruger.

ISBN: 978-3-7913-5527-6

CONTENTS

Robert Mapplethorpe, **Portrait of Eli Broad**, 1987, black-and-white photograph, 24 x 20 in. (60.9 x 50.8 cm)

Robert Mapplethorpe, **Portrait of Edythe Broad**, 1987, black-and-white photograph, 24 x 20 in. (60.9 x 50.8 cm)

INTRODUCTION TO THE BROAD COLLECTION

JOANNE HEYLER

The art collection of The Broad emerges from Eli and Edythe Broad's enthusiasm for collecting that began in the early 1960s. While overseeing the formation and expansion of two rapidly growing businesses, Eli satisfied an innate appetite for wider interests through his passion for art. He and his wife pursued art and collecting not only as an enriching avocation, but also as an opportunity to give back to the community. Over the past four decades, the Broads have built one of the most prominent collections of postwar and contemporary art worldwide, including nearly 2,000 works by more than 200 artists.

Eli and Edye grew up in an America both ripe with economic prosperity as well as anxiety about its role in an increasingly volatile globalized world. They attended public schools, including in Eli's case Michigan State University, where he graduated early and became the state's youngest ever CPA at the age of 19. They were married in 1954. Eli's precocious launch of a housing development company in his twenties—which he quickly moved from Detroit to L.A.—began a stunning five-decade business career in which he became the first corporate CEO in history to create two Fortune 500 companies in two different industries.

The collection the Broads have built emerges from the American postwar period and exemplifies the forces and phenomena that have shaped much of the art produced in this time. No collection can cover every artist, style, or movement, but the best ones, whether institutional or personal, tell an essential piece of an unbounded and living story of art. The Broad collection tells its own particular version of the story of contemporary art. The Broads' biographies echo the American postwar period in essential ways, from their Midwestern childhoods in the industrial powerhouse that was midcentury Detroit, to the housing and financial industries definitive of the mid to late 20th-century American economy in which Eli became a business leader.

While the Broads' interest in contemporary art began primarily as a personal pursuit, it expanded quickly to become a focal point of their public philanthropy. The Broad Art Foundation was established in 1984 by the Broads to foster public appreciation of contemporary art by increasing access for audiences worldwide. The Foundation's active loan program makes works available for exhibition at arts institutions through-out the world. Since its creation, the Foundation has made more than 8,000 loans to over 500 museums. The Broad now operates as both a museum and a headquarters for The Broad Art Foundation's lending library of artworks, ensuring that the collection is accessible to the widest possible public through an array of international exhibition venues as well as its home base at The Broad.

The Broad collection is diverse, but it has distinct abiding emphases. A strong current of socially and politically themed art

Sharon Lockhart, **Lunch Break Installation, "Duane Hanson: Sculptures of Life,"** 14 December 2002–23 February 2003, Scottish National Gallery of Modern Art, 2003, four chromogenic prints, each 72 x 121 in. (182.8 x 307.3 cm)

in the collection dovetails with the Broads' activist attitude toward philanthropy in social welfare issues ranging from public schools to medical research; the emphasis on figuration indicates an attraction to the concrete, the here and now, and less engagement with the purely conceptual. Their long history of collecting contemporary German art—an interest they shared with several American collector peers in the 1980s—connects to one of the central, defining episodes of their generation: the recovery of Germany from the ravages of World War II.

A hallmark of the collection is the exceptional depth of its holdings of works by numerous major figures of the postwar and contemporary periods, including Jean-Michel Basquiat, Joseph Beuys, Damien Hirst, Anselm Kiefer, Jeff Koons, Barbara Kruger, Roy Lichtenstein, Sharon Lockhart, Ed Ruscha, Cindy Sherman, Cy Twombly, Kara Walker, and Andy Warhol.

Jeff Koons, Installation view of **Tulips**, 1995–2004, and **Balloon Dog (Blue)**, 1994–2000, in the exhibition *Re-object*, Kunsthaus Bregenz, February 2007

THE BUILDING

The Broad was designed by New York–based architects Diller Scofidio + Renfro (DS+R), in collaboration with Gensler, and is DS+R's first project in Los Angeles. Their design was conceived to complement downtown L.A.'s distinguished stretch of architecturally significant buildings along Grand Avenue, and specifically to create a visual dialogue with Walt Disney Concert Hall, designed by noted L.A. architect Frank Gehry. DS+R's design is tailored to the art in the Broad collection and to the Broad collection's long history as an institution dedicated to lending its artworks to museums around the world.

     The architects chose to put at center stage The Broad's back-of-house functions—the areas where its artworks are maintained, stored, and conserved—by placing the "vault" at the heart of the building, making it, as lead architect Elizabeth Diller has said, "the protagonist" of their unusual design. Connecting

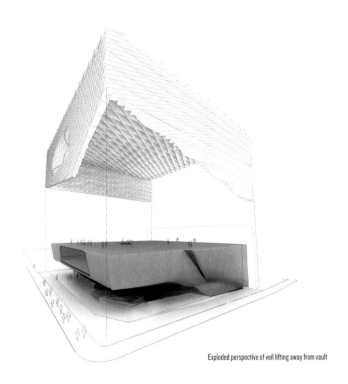

Exploded perspective of veil lifting away from vault

The Broad lobby escalator to main galleries

the exhibition levels on the first and third floors of the building is an enclosed escalator and a cylindrical glass elevator that tunnel through collection storage. From select vantage points on the third and second floors, as well as during the egress down the central stairs, one can glimpse views through large plate-glass windows into the "pre-curated" art situated on racks and shelves in the storage area around which the museum is built.

The Broad as seen from Grand Avenue with Disney Hall adjacent

This porosity down into the museum's very core begins with the building's outermost structure, the "veil." When one drives or walks by The Broad, its torqued, lattice-like veil functions as an architectural invitation to the viewing of art. A distinctive pattern of apertures puncture the veil at carefully calibrated angles that leave it ambiguously situated between solidity and transparency. Once inside, visitors experience the

Facade of The Broad with oculus

Broad collection in concert with the building's dynamic design, while remaining connected to the outside and to the street, even from the third-floor galleries, via momentary oblique glimpses through the veil structure. The Broad is a tribute to DS+R's investigation of what it means to observe contemporary life while also being observed, and to their long commitment to studying the dynamics of looking. The creation of a pedestrian-friendly plaza on the museum's south side also adds social vibrancy along the avenue.

The Broad provides a counterpoint to neighboring Disney Hall, one of the great architectural masterpieces of our time. The Broad's light-absorbing exterior, including its dramatic skylights, filter light gently into the building for the purpose of illuminating the art, in contrast to Disney's deflection of the surrounding urban environment away from the suspended reality of its performance space. The Broad therefore sits, its perforated white surface almost mineral-like and static, as an intriguingly internalized structure complementing rather than competing with the exuberance of Disney's massive, dancing steel-clad forms.

Beyond Gehry's transformational contribution, The Broad extends a growing list of significant Grand Avenue architecture. It joins The Music Center by Welton Becket (1964–67), the Museum of Contemporary Art, Los Angeles by Arata Isozaki (1986), The Colburn School by Hardy Holzman Pfeiffer Associates (1998), the Cathedral of Our Lady of the Angels by Rafael Moneo (2002), and the Ramón C. Cortines School of the Visual and Performing Arts (2008) by Wolfgang Prix of Coop Himmelb(l)au. The scope of art and culture that can be experienced today on Grand Avenue is unmatched anywhere else in L.A. The design of The Broad deliberately departs from the majority of its architectural neighbors, who, through entryways set high on plinths above the street, or set low on decking beneath street level, have disconnected themselves from the essential urban pedestrian experience. The Broad's dramatic lobby at sidewalk level, and its veil lifted at its corners welcomes and connects to passersby. Its green plaza to the south, also designed by DS+R, which The Broad can use for public programming, is also contiguous with the streetscape. Furthermore, neighboring restaurants and residential buildings engage with The Broad's plaza and bring the prospect of Grand Avenue as a place which can be experienced beyond isolated cultural encounters. With the design of The Broad, DS+R has encouraged a more nuanced, pedestrian-friendly Grand Avenue, where people can live, dine and enjoy a dynamic urban environment day or night, inside and outside, throughout the year.

Aerial view of The Broad and downtown Los Angeles

COLLECTION HIGHLIGHTS

JOHN BALDESSARI

Tips for Artists Who Want to Sell, 1966–68
Acrylic on canvas
68 ¼ x 56 ½ in. (173.3 x 143.5 cm)

John Baldessari never touched this painting. He did not paint it.
He did not write the text. "There is a certain kind of work one
could do that didn't require a studio," Baldessari said, "It's work
that is done in one's head. The artist could be the facilitator of
the work; executing it was another matter." This concept—that
an artist could present an idea rather than a material object from
their own hand—was a way for Baldessari to take apart the
notion of what art could be. In 1966, art meant painting, sculpture, or drawing, and with wry humor, Baldessari challenges this
expectation. The viewer receives a painting in *Tips for Artists Who
Want to Sell*, but the painting is completed by sign painters. The
viewer is presented with a painting's content, but the content is
text taken from an art trade magazine dictating what content
should be. Baldessari disperses art's alleged essence, casting a net
far beyond what "sells" and what art history dictates.

TIPS FOR ARTISTS
WHO WANT TO SELL

• GENERALLY SPEAKING, PAINT-
INGS WITH LIGHT COLORS SELL
MORE QUICKLY THAN PAINTINGS
WITH DARK COLORS.

• SUBJECTS THAT SELL WELL:
MADONNA AND CHILD, LANDSCAPES,
FLOWER PAINTINGS, STILL LIFES
(FREE OF MORBID PROPS ＿＿＿
DEAD BIRDS, ETC.), NUDES, MARINE
PICTURES, ABSTRACTS AND SUR-
REALISM.

• SUBJECT MATTER IS IMPOR -
TANT: IT HAS BEEN SAID THAT PA-
INTINGS WITH COWS AND HENS
IN THEM COLLECT DUST
＿＿＿ WHILE THE SAME PAINTINGS
WITH BULLS AND ROOSTERS SELL.

JEAN-MICHEL BASQUIAT

Untitled, 1981
Acrylic and oilstick on canvas
81 x 69¼ in. (205.7 x 175.8 cm)

Many of Jean-Michel Basquiat's paintings are in some way
autobiographical, and *Untitled* is largely considered a form of
self-portraiture. The skull exists somewhere between life and
death. The eyes are listless, the face is sunken in, and the head
looks lobotomized and subdued. Yet, there are wild colors and
spirited marks that suggest a surfeit of internal activity.
Developing his personal iconography, in this early work, Basquiat
both alludes to modernist appropriation of African masks and
employs the mask as a means of exploring identity. Basquiat
labored over this painting for months—evident in the worked
surface and imagery—while most of his pieces were completed
with bursts of energy over a few days. Presented at his debut solo
gallery exhibition in New York City, the intensity of the painting
may also represent Basquiat's anxieties surrounding the pres-
sures of becoming a commercially successful artist.

BERND AND HILLA BECHER

Water Towers, 1972
Two of six suites of nine black-and-white photographs
Each suite 52 ⅝ x 40 ⅝ in. (133.6 x 103.1 cm) overall

Bernd and Hilla Becher document nondescript industrial buildings such as smokestacks, water towers, and factories. The
Bechers used a large-format camera placed at a raised vantage
point and allowed a long exposure time to give distant structures

crisp, chiseled, sculptural detail. Their subjects show neither human activity nor the splendor of the landscape, though they passively point to both. The photographs capture a fading world, an architectural moment after World War II when the old industrial structure of Germany gave way to the surging needs of a newly robust economy. In their collaborative career, the Bechers completed over 200 comprehensive documentary collections, each ranging from 50 to 100 images. In this typology, the Bechers monumentalize and categorize the various forms constructed for storing water, each designed and built with their own idiosyncrasies while generally remaining the same.

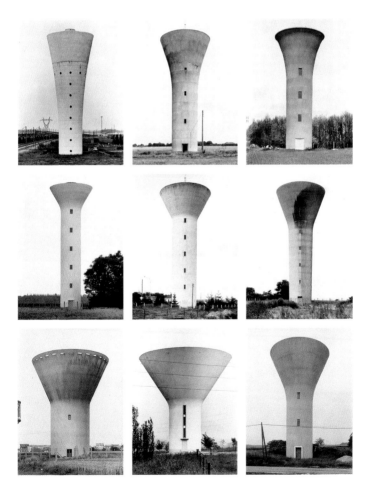

JOSEPH BEUYS

Schlitten, 1969
Wood sled stamped with oil paint (Browncross), felt, belts, flashlight, fat, and rope
13 11/16 x 35 3/8 x 13 11/16 in. (34.7 x 89.8 x 34.7 cm)

Actively contributing to *Vergangenheitsbewältigung*, the 1960s German movement that addressed the nation's fascist history, Joseph Beuys created mythologies as a means to comprehend a discordant past. *Schlitten* consists of a wooden sled equipped with a flashlight, belts, rope, felt, and fat. The sculpture is stamped with Browncross, a neutral household paint that appears in many of the artist's multiples. Playing into the artist's autobiographical

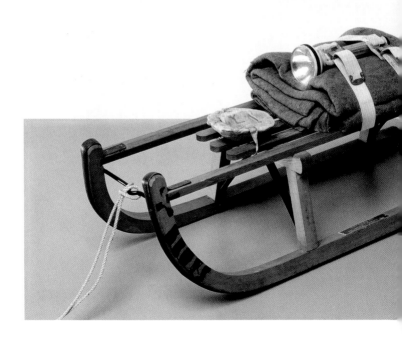

myth, *Schlitten* transports its viewer to the Crimean scene where Beuys's plane is storied to have crashed during World War II. Rescued by a band of Tartars, he was wrapped in felt and fat. The tale is one of rebirth, of survival and healing, and the work itself is at once a symbol of decay and restoration. Whether fact or fiction, the poignant tale is both personal and universal.

MARK BRADFORD

Corner of Desire and Piety, 2008
Mixed media collage
Overall approx. 135 ¾ x 344 ¼ in. (344.8 x 874.3 cm)

Mark Bradford's *Corner of Desire and Piety* is so large, repetitive,
and monochromatic that it behaves like a wall or blockade. The
opaque silver surface initially deflects viewers from its impene-
trable field; the text, however, creates an opening that reveals the
work's true magnitude. Each of the 72 panels announces the
delivery of propane intended for FEMA trailers in New Orleans.
The work reflects the conundrum many residents faced after
Hurricane Katrina when such deliveries were exploited by some

for profit. They had to make a choice: fulfill their own needs while making some extra cash or patiently suffer along with everyone else. Though the actual streets in New Orleans named Desire and Piety run parallel through the Lower Ninth Ward, the predominantly black neighborhood devastated by the flooding, Bradford forges a metaphorical intersection—a painful choice—stoked by the tragedy of Katrina.

ALEXANDER CALDER

The S-Shaped Vine, 1946
Painted sheet metal and wire
98½ x 79 in. (250.1 x 200.6 cm)

Bringing movement to the medium of sculpture, Alexander
Calder is one of the most influential artists of the 20th century.
Calder's mobiles, the solution to his quest for motion in art, are
meditations in metal, wire, and steel, eloquent in their abilities
to move and shift while hanging from stands or ceilings. Earlier
in his career, Calder sought to maintain control over the direc-
tion and speed of his kinetic sculptures, carefully planning the
elements that would balance and align in predetermined ways.
But as his art progressed, he became more interested in allowing
his work to catch chance impulses. The experience of a Calder
mobile is always subtle and new, and the sculpture's true instinct
is to represent the variations in movement of a set number of
shapes within the changing conditions of a gallery.

CHUCK CLOSE

John, 1971–72
Acrylic on canvas
100 x 90 in. (254 x 228.6 cm)

Chuck Close is known as much for his detailed representation of the human face as for his subsequent deconstruction of it. Close uses head-on portraits as his templates, exploring the portrait form itself through a variety of drawing and painterly techniques, as well as through printmaking, tapestry, and photography. *John*, one of Close's earliest paintings, is described as photorealist. Indeed, Close refers to photographs to create his artworks, employing their inconsistencies of perspective as much as their verisimilitude. Here, the sharp detail of the rim of the subject's glasses contrasts with the blurred, soft focus of his shoulders and the back of his hair, as it likely did in the original photograph. But instead of using mechanical means to transfer his images onto canvas, Close works entirely from sight to achieve the intensely animate detail, sectioning off the reference photographs into grids and transferring them by hand onto his monumentally sized canvases.

JOHN CURRIN

Patch and Pearl, 2006
Oil on canvas
80 x 50 in (203.2 x 127 cm)

In *Patch and Pearl*, John Currin portrays two apparently pregnant women who are almost alien in their forms: lean on top and extremely fecund below the waist. Standing on a rooftop, the two women look out hopefully, as if awaiting the return—from war perhaps—of the fathers of their unborn children. The home-grown American optimism on their faces rivals that in a Norman Rockwell painting, yet their distended bellies tell a different story: this is not exactly a return to peaceful times and conventional family values. Pearl carries her baby like a growth; it is lumpy and sagging. Patch may be wearing her pants backward; strange things have happened since the men have been away. With the rooflines bisecting the canvas twice, even the composition is unsettling. The bizarre and the banal go hand in hand in this town, and the effect to an outsider is disquieting.

SAM FRANCIS

Big Orange, 1954–55
Oil on canvas
118 ¼ x 76 in. (300.3 x 193 cm)

Sam Francis moved to Paris from the California Bay Area in the
early 1950s. Francis was inspired by Paris, by Claude Monet's
water lilies, and Pierre Bonnard's windblown leaves and outdoor
tabletops. He transmuted many of the interests of the impres-
sionists into a contemporary vocabulary, aiming to capture the
fleeting wonder of everyday light and movement through a
patchwork of pigment. *Big Orange* evokes moving clouds or the
shimmering surface of water, perhaps even a thick Pacific fog
rolling into San Francisco Bay. The presence of overlapping black
and white borders of paint surrounding the impacted orange
surface is especially important. Francis's experiments with
borders and the containment of washes of color would inform his
work for decades, as he became increasingly concerned with the
respresentation of solids and voids, boundaries and fields.

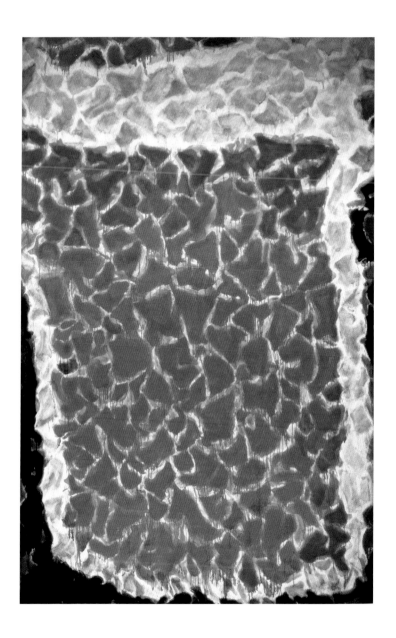

ANDREAS GURSKY

99 Cent, 1999
Chromogenic print mounted on Plexiglas in artist's frame
81 ½ x 132 ⅝ in. (207 x 336.8 cm)

A student of conceptual photographers Bernd and Hilla Becher, Andreas Gursky takes an ordered, indexical approach to his work. Capturing scenes with enormous amounts of visual information, Gursky subtly enhances and adjusts the structure of his photographs, enabling viewers to assimilate and consume more than is possible with their eyes alone. *99 Cent* is a clear example of Gursky's alteration of images for a totalizing effect. Modifications such as the arrangement of the store's product aisles and the

mirrored roof flatten the iconic work. The spectacle of consumerism appears composed in an organized, rigorous, formal fashion.
The presented image is hyperreal; while it is rooted in reality, it
is somehow more than real, it is familiar and yet there is no
physical space quite like it. By portraying such heightened
constructions of our shared existence, from the dollar store to
the soccer field to the sprawling cityscape, Gursky's photographs
act as symbols of contemporary life.

DAMIEN HIRST

Away from the Flock, 1994
Glass, painted steel, silicone, acrylic, plastic, lamb, and formaldehyde solution
37 ¾ x 58 ⅝ x 20 in. (95.8 x 148.9 x 50.8 cm)

As a prominent member of the Young British Artists group, Damien Hirst has had a significant and prolific career since the late 1980s. Developing a visual language that combines scientific processes with Christian iconography, Hirst works in sculpture, installation, painting, and printmaking. He creates art that confronts essential conditions of the human experience, namely the realities and rituals surrounding death, desire, and fear. *Away from the Flock* features a lifeless sheep suspended in formaldehyde

within a glass-walled tank. By using formaldehyde, Hirst references scientific study that attempts to preserve once living material. The sheep on display represents the limits of preservation, its inability to evade death. The sculpture's title uses religious terminology to suggest a similar failure. The work forces us to address our own ultimate mortality, resulting in emotional, empathetic responses.

JASPER JOHNS

Flag, 1967
Encaustic and collage on canvas, three panels
Overall 33 ⅛ x 56 in. (84.1 x 142.2 cm)

"One night I dreamed that I painted a large American flag," Jasper Johns has said, "and the next morning I got up and I went out and bought the materials to begin it." It is a simple origin story for a group of paintings that have become among the touchstones of recent art history. The American flag is both an abstraction of an idea and a symbol, but what does the flag become when it is painted? Is it an image of the object or the object itself? Johns's *Flag* is a perceptual game, a two-step between reality and illusion that extends to the meaning of the work. Produced at the height of the Cold War, Johns's take on the flag is analytic, cool, and unsentimental.

JASPER JOHNS

Watchman, 1964
Oil on canvas with objects, two panels
Overall 85 x 60¼ in. (215.9 x 175.8 cm)

Watchman was made while Jasper Johns was living abroad in Tokyo in 1964. The seminal work features a wax cast of Johns's friend's leg, two canvas panels, and half of a standard dining table chair. The surface of the painting is seemingly in the midst of action. The words "red," "yellow," and "blue" printed partially on the left side of the canvas appear as though in a state of erasure, while their colorful pigment counterparts appear (also disrupted) on the right. The inversion of the chair upward to the sky leaves an aftermath of orange, green, and gray, like a falling rain of expressive marks across a once ordered surface. Overall, *Watchman* is a painting that is trying to be more than a painting; it is caught in the very moment where the world of thought and representation (of symbols and signs) is transitioning into the world of action and physical expression.

ELLSWORTH KELLY

Green Blue Red, 1963
Oil on canvas
67 ½ x 90 in. (171.4 x 228.6 cm)

Throughout the late 1950s and early 60s, Ellsworth Kelly worked with shapes and solid colors deployed flatly across single canvases. Finding inspiration in both nature and art, he was drawn to the oddity of forms and the various conditions that create visual interest in unlikely ways. In this spirit, _Green Blue Red_

eschews the balance and harmony of traditional painting and reflects an impulse to build a surface of visual tension out of the contrasts of color and shape and the containment of an edge. Kelly's works of this period were also influenced by the strange visual style of Romanesque painters, who often crowded saints and dramatic narrative scenes into small pendentives. As the characters push out against the edges of the allotted spaces in chapels and crypts, here the green rectangle and the blue oval push out of the respective edges of a red field. The jarring difference between the colors and the unusual placement of the shapes energize the visual experience and create a disorienting optical effect.

WILLIAM KENTRIDGE

Installation views of *The Refusal of Time*, 2012
A collaboration with Philip Miller, Catherine Meyburgh, and Peter Galison
Five-channel video installation, sound, 30 min.; four steel megaphones;
and breathing machine ("elephant")

The films of William Kentridge are based in drawing and collage.
Beginning with an original charcoal drawing, the artist moves
pieces of cut-up or torn paper within the work, then erases and
redraws in a process that is repeated many times. The incremen-
tal changes to the picture are captured with a camera, frame by
frame, and the residue of previous images fades slowly as new
imagery emerges. The resulting film is less a traditional anima-
tion and more a series of fluidly moving drawings that tell a
fantastical story rich with personal, political, and historical
allegory. *The Refusal of Time* is a gallery-size, multipart installation
that includes an original score, a large kinetic sculpture, and
multiple film projections. The work is an exploration of the
history and unraveling of time. Kentridge, in reference to this
piece, described how "time itself had to give up—just as perfect
time was thought to be possible, it was proven to be impossible."
For Kentridge, there is freedom in imperfection, disorder, and
chaos. The messy epistemological conditions to which humans
must adapt in order to survive provide the engine for creativity,
optimism, and ultimately, beauty.

ANSELM KIEFER

Deutschlands Geisteshelden, 1973
Oil and charcoal on burlap mounted on canvas
120 ½ x 267 ¾ in. (306 x 680 cm)

Born at the close of World War II, Anselm Kiefer reflects upon
and critiques the myths and chauvinism that propelled the
German Third Reich to power. With immense scale and ambition,
his paintings depict his generation's ambivalence toward the
grandiose impulse of German nationalism and its impact on
history. Painted in extreme perspective, *Deutschlands Geisteshelden*
positions the viewer at the mouth of a great hall, an amalgam of
Kiefer's former studio and Carinhall, a German hunting lodge
used to store looted art during the Nazi era. Burning torches line
the walls of the space, which is empty except for the names of

inspirational artists and writers scrawled above the receding floor: Joseph Beuys, Arnold Böcklin, Adalbert Stifter, Caspar David Friedrich, Theodor Strom, and many others. This is hardly a hall of gods or a triumphal place, however, the lodge keeps vigil, housing names that have become embroiled and perhaps tainted by history. Even the greatest ideas fell into shadow in the wake of the atrocities of the Third Reich.

RAGNAR KJARTANSSON

Still from *The Visitors*, 2012
Nine-channel HD video installation, sound, 64 min. loop
Sound: Chris McDonald
Video: Tómas Örn Tómasson

Icelandic artist Ragnar Kjartansson's nine-screen installation
The Visitors was filmed at the historic Rokeby farm in upstate
New York. Kjartansson invited a group of friends to stay with him
for a week at the ethereal, decrepit estate, culminating in the
ambitious performance. The title references the Swedish pop
band ABBA's final album of the same name, suggesting parallels
between the contents of and the social conditions surrounding
the works. Running for over an hour, *The Visitors* was produced in
one take, recording each musician's performance simultaneously

in different rooms of the mansion. The friends play the same song, instilling it with nuanced meaning through voice, instrument, and movements of the body. Kjartansson himself plays much of his rendition in a bathtub. The installation elicits feeling through duration and repetition: rituals are personalized, subtle variations emerge and decay. The lyrics are based on a poem by Ásdís Sif Gunnarsdóttir and the musical arrangements are by Kjartansson and Davíð Þór Jónsson.

JEFF KOONS

Rabbit, 1986
Stainless steel
41 x 19 x 12 in. (104.1 x 48.2 x 30.4 cm)

In 1979 Jeff Koons made The Broad collection's *Inflatable Flower and Bunny (Tall White, Pink Bunny)*, a pivotal work in the artist's early career. The sculpture features two vinyl inflatable toys—a flower and a pink bunny—that sit on top and in front of four square mirrors. Seven years later, Koons ditched the flower, combined the mirror and the bunny, and made *Rabbit*. The switch from the word "bunny" to "rabbit" is intriguing. Bunny is cute and floppy; rabbit is quick and sharp. The carrot in the rabbit's paw is wielded like a weapon, and the once soft, leaky, and cheap vinyl shell of the bunny has been replaced by armorlike, costly stainless steel, which reflects everything surrounding the rabbit and deflects any allusions to the sculpture's interior.

JEFF KOONS

Michael Jackson and Bubbles, 1988
Porcelain
42 x 70½ x 32½ in. (106.6 x 179 x 82.5 cm)

In his Banality series, Jeff Koons creates sculptures of recognizable cultural figures and images, from stuffed animals to celebrity magazine photos, addressing wide-ranging audiences. In *Michael Jackson and Bubbles*, Koons plays with the notion of kitsch, basing the work on a photograph of the infamous pop star and his pet chimpanzee. Cast in porcelain and painted gold, the sculpture resembles a souvenir figurine. The oversized scale of

the work, however, sets it apart from the objects it mimics. Fabricated by an Italian craftsman who makes traditional ornamental and religious items, the resulting sculpture recalls works of the Renaissance, namely Michelangelo's *Pietà*. With *Michael Jackson and Bubbles*, Koons strongly asserts the comparison between religious icon and cultural idol.

BARBARA KRUGER

Untitled (Your body is a battleground), 1989
Photographic silkscreen on vinyl
112 x 112 in. (284.4 x 284.4 cm)

Barbara Kruger addresses media and politics in their native tongue with sensational, authoritative, and direct works. Kruger's words and images merge the commercial and art worlds; their critical resonance eviscerates cultural hierarchies—everyone and everything is for sale. The year 1989 was marked by numerous demonstrations protesting a new wave of anti-abortion laws chipping away at the 1973 Roe v. Wade Supreme Court decision. _Untitled (Your body is a battleground)_ was produced by Kruger for the Women's March on Washington in support of reproductive freedom. The woman's face, disembodied, bisected in positive and negative exposures, and obscured by text, marks a stark divide. This image is simultaneously art and protest; though its origin is tied to a specific moment, the power of the work lies in the timelessness of its declaration.

YAYOI KUSAMA

Infinity Mirrored Room—The Souls of Millions of Light Years Away, 2013
Wood, metal, glass mirrors, plastic, acrylic panel, rubber, LED lighting system, acrylic balls, and water
113 ¼ x 163 ½ x 163 ½ in. (288.2 x 415. 2 x 415.2 cm)

Yayoi Kusama's notable career spans over half a century; her multidisciplinary art practice includes painting, performance, installation, writing, film, fashion, design, and architectural interventions. Moving between modes of working, Kusama has eluded associations with specific art movements and instead she has developed a unique brand. Her famed dot motif is internationally recognized and is on full display in *Infinity Mirrored Room—The Souls of Millions of Light Years Away*, an immersive installation with LED lights reflecting endlessly in the mirrored space. Since the 1960s, Kusama has been creating Infinity Mirrored Rooms that provoke a mentality of boundlessness through extreme repetition. Kusama's work is an expression of her life, providing insight into the many social and political contexts of her long career. Through her artwork, Kusama, a self-proclaimed "obsessional artist," offers an unusual glimpse into the workings of a mind that is seldom quiet. The strength and universal appeal of her work goes beyond stylistic design: Kusama confronts the immensity of reality by searching at once for infinitude and oblivion.

SHERRIE LEVINE

Fountain (Buddha), 1996
Cast bronze
12 x 15 ⅞ x 18 in. (30.4 x 40.3 x 45.7 cm)

Sherrie Levine, along with artists such as Robert Longo, Richard Prince, David Salle, and Cindy Sherman, is often labeled as part of the pictures generation. Coined by critic Douglas Crimp in 1977, the title defined how the concerns of photography fed into and informed painting and sculpture. Levine's work was central to Crimp's claims, especially her use of editions and copies to undermine long-sacred beliefs of originality in art. Levine copied famous works directly, reprinting photography and remaking sculptures. The pioneer of this idea was Marcel Duchamp, whose 1917 *Fountain*, a standard urinal put on display in an art exhibition, bluntly demanded to be either disproven or approved as "art." *Fountain (Buddha)* is Levine's homage to Duchamp's renowned readymade. Adding to his audacious artistic move, she turned his gesture back into an "art object" by elevating its materiality and finish. The concept is that once the meaning of an object transcends the artist's intent, then the purpose and definition of the artwork can be explored and critiqued by other artists.

ROY LICHTENSTEIN

I...I'm Sorry, 1965–66
Oil and Magna on canvas
60 x 48 in. (152.4 x 121.9 cm)

Though Roy Lichtenstein's style of comic-derived pop art is now
well known, it was radical in the early 1960s. Appropriating the
visual language of American mass culture, such as Mickey Mouse,
Coca-Cola, and the "funny pages," Lichtenstein found his artistic
voice by making paintings that at first did not appear to be art.
This was his cover—part camouflage and part red herring—which
allowed him to insert his own practice into the art historical
milieu; he was in dialogue with the greats, reprising themes from
antiquity. *I...I'm Sorry* is a portrait of Eve as a modern-day woman.
Lichtenstein renders her apology unclear, revealing layers of
interpretation: is she apologizing for eating the forbidden fruit
from the tree? Is she breaking our hearts? Is she sincere with her
stammering words? Her simplified features belie the nuanced
complexities of her declaration.

GLENN LIGON

Double America 2, 2014
Neon and paint
48 x 145 x 3 in. (121.9 x 368.3 x 7.6 cm)

Glenn Ligon's early love of literature evolved into a fascination
with the political and social uses of language and the ways in
which art can exploit and repurpose the written word. Ligon
coaxes complex and often contradictory meanings from texts as
they are presented in his paintings, prints, and sculptures,
especially as they apply to the formation and perception of

identity and race. In *Double America 2*, Ligon uses black paint to eclipse the glow of neon. Instead of throwing light forward, the neon illuminates the wall behind it, and dark shadows trace the path of the tubing on the wall. The work consists of two signs that spell America: one is upright and the other is upside down. Though identical, the mere flipping of one perverts the entire composition. The signs are separate but linked; the doubling does not compound the meaning, it disperses it. Pundits often refer to a "black America" and a "white America," as if the country were a binary. Here, Ligon poetically acknowledges multiple, interconnected experiences of America. Mirroring, aligning, illuminating, doubling, shadowing, and eclipsing, each action informs the others as it asserts itself.

JULIE MEHRETU

Cairo, 2013
Ink and acrylic on canvas
120 x 288 in. (304.8 x 731.5 cm)

In her monumental paintings, Julie Mehretu begins with a
structure—schools, airports, government buildings—upon which
to anchor her frenetic mark-making and precise renderings
culled from archival sources. *Cairo* presents the ancient Egyptian
city caught in a furious wind blowing off the Sahara, its structures and history extending into black and white vectors.
Simultaneously, the work portrays Cairo as a contemporary,
revolutionary city in the political spotlight, raising the world's

consciousness about government suppression and citizen-led change. The enormous work registers as a physical force, asserting itself as one unified mass. However, it also contains a level of detail that creates strong individual moments on the canvas. *Cairo* embodies dichotomies: ancient and contemporary, social and political, mass and individual. It is an expression of a city's life and the complexity of its continued existence.

TAKASHI MURAKAMI

In the Land of the Dead, Stepping on the Tail of a Rainbow, 2014
Acrylic on canvas
118 ⅛ x 984 ¼ in. (300 x 2500 cm)

Takashi Murakami's massive 82-foot-long painting, *In the Land of the Dead, Stepping on the Tail of a Rainbow*, is informed by 18th-century painters Soga Shohaku and Ito Jakuchu. Shohaku believed in reaching for new and alternative truths in picture making by imitating existing forms or styles and imbuing them with new essence. Murakami follows this belief, here using figures and motifs directly taken from Shohaku's painting *Gunsenzu*, or *Immortals* (1764), itself an imitation of an older

version, which depicts Taoist hermits with magical powers. On the far left, a hermit in blue riding a dragon; the hermit on the far right who holds a baby; and the potbellied hermit leaning on a frog are but a few motifs Murakami appropriates from *Immortals*. However, the painting is unmistakably Murakami's, reminiscent of contemporary Japanese cartooning and culture though rooted in centuries-old traditions.

LARI PITTMAN

Like You, 1995
Oil and enamel on five mahogany panels
Overall 96 x 320 in. (243.8 x 812.8 cm)

This monumentally sized work is comprised of five panels. Lari
Pittman has filled up the painting, flattening perspective and
making each panel sparkle with activity. By bringing everything
to the surface, Pittman creates a device enabling multiple layers
of imagery. Pittman's work does not easily break down into
typical binaries, and here he actively seeks to disrupt them. The
imagery is both interior and exterior, decorative and narrative,
graphic and painterly. The work depicts an event in full swing—
an upheaval of order, perhaps a riot or a parade with androgy-
nous thong-wearing revelers and hands either praying or
clapping. The scale and amount of imagery in Pittman's painting
are aggressively magnanimous. Rendered in exquisite detail, the
overflowing canvas presents nuanced complexities.

ROBERT RAUSCHENBERG

Untitled, 1954
Oil, fabric, and newspaper on canvas
70 ¾ x 47 in. (179.7 x 121.6 cm)

Robert Rauschenberg had a voracious appetite for material
culture and for getting that culture into works of art. A collage of
wood, newspaper, comics, sundry clothes, and old lace, *Untitled* is
saturated with a thick sealing coat of red paint. The surface is
open to drips and chance combinations, not with an expressive
intent as in abstract expressionism but instead as a field of
unexpected juxtapositions and perceptual shifts. *Untitled* is an
important step in Rauschenberg's development as an artist; his
use of everyday objects would continue to evolve, eventually
producing a hybrid of painting and sculpture now known as the
Combine paintings. This is also an important artwork for Eli and
Edythe Broad. When they acquired *Untitled*, the Broads sold
Vincent van Gogh's drawing *Cabanes à Saintes-Maries*, 1888, which
they had cherished for a long time. For the Broads, the acquisi-
tion of *Untitled* in 1983 was a turning point in their life as
collectors, a symbol of their increasing commitment to the works
of contemporary artists.

CHARLES RAY

Firetruck, 1993
Painted aluminum, fiberglass, and Plexiglas
144 x 558 x 96 in. (365.7 x 1417.3 x 243.8 cm)

Often playing with scale, Charles Ray exposes the psychological
implications of an object's size in relation to the human body. His
monumental sculpture *Firetruck* is a toy fire engine fabricated to
the dimensions of a functioning one. It was created for the 1993
Whitney Biennial and installed on Madison Avenue in front of

the museum. Though the scale of the truck makes it appear serviceable, the painted-on valves, gauges, hoses, and ladders reveal its nonutilitarian status. Ray's sculpture evokes the drama of adult-size calamities while maintaining childlike optimism and imagination. The fantasies of young and old mix together allowing for the child's vision of heroism and power as well as the adult's desire for play and a yet undeveloped sense of mortality. The architecture surrounding *Firetruck* takes on equally sculptural and constructed qualities. The sculpture calls attention to the buildings and infrastructure that started small—as models—and were built large.

ED RUSCHA

Norm's, La Cienega, on Fire, 1964
Oil and pencil on canvas
64 ½ x 124 ¾ in. (163.8 x 316.8 cm)

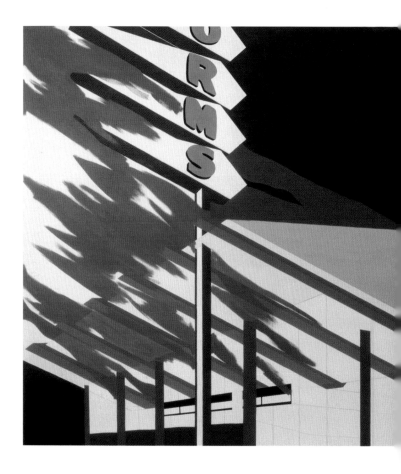

Norm's diner is a roadside icon, one of a number of 24-hour restaurants that populate Southern California, slinging pancakes to paying customers. For Ed Ruscha, Norm's carried the same graphic status as the Hollywood sign, the titles at the beginning of movies, or the bright gas station signs of the Standard Oil Company, all of which became subjects for the artist's work in the 1960s, all symbols of the American landscape, atmosphere,

and even the particular idiom of English that Americans speak. *Norm's, La Cienega, on Fire* is the first painting by Ruscha of a building set ablaze. The fire brings a surreal edge burning with an almost comic enthusiasm, a moment of expressive energy and even melodrama in a clean, well-lit 1960s world.

CINDY SHERMAN

Untitled Film Still #06, 1977
Gelatin silver print
10 x 8 in. (25.4 x 20.3 cm)

Untitled Film Still #54, 1980
Gelatin silver print
8 x 10 in. (20.3 x 25.4 cm)

In the *Untitled Film Stills*, the archetypal characters that Cindy Sherman appropriates through her own acting, costuming, and photography highlight the relationship between consumerism and personal identity. Taking cues from filmic tropes, Sherman compounds fact and fiction, literally trying on an assortment of personalities and circumstances as if they were hats. Ultimately, Sherman's work points to the slippery nature of identity and the conflict of equating outward appearance with the essence of being human. Sherman's characters embody and critique social norms of beauty at the same time. In 1982, Eli and Edythe Broad first encountered Sherman's *Untitled Film Stills*. The theatricality and typological approach of the works had a profound effect on the Broads, who acquired 20 photographs by the relatively unknown young artist that same day. The Broad's collection of Sherman's work has steadily been among the most committed and deep holdings of the artist's work worldwide.

ROBERT THERRIEN

Under the Table, 1994
Wood, metal, and enamel
117 x 312 x 216 in. (297.1 x 792.4 x 548.6 cm)

Robert Therrien's objects are very familiar. They are ordinary
items—tables, chairs, plates, pitchers, keyholes, and even
snowmen—transported with care across media, scales, and
environments. Derived from the artist's experiences, the objects
are more than personal symbols, they are products of a collective
memory. We have seen these pieces before, but not in quite the

same way that Therrien has seen them. This oddity of vision makes his objects both new and strikingly nostalgic. In *Under the Table*, Therrien fuses *Alice's Adventures in Wonderland* with the Duchampian tradition of the readymade. Constructing a doppel-gänger from an everyday piece of furniture, he both displays his visual wit and actualizes literary or imaginative fantasy in three-dimensional space. The table, at nearly ten feet tall, exudes an extraordinary presence. One is compelled to walk underneath it, conjuring up the memory of what it felt like to be under the table as a small child. Complicated and powerful, the work taps into one's consciousness, using scale to summon recollections as a familiar fragrance or flavor might.

CY TWOMBLY

Untitled [New York City], 1953
Oil-based house paint and wax crayon on canvas
52 x 52 in. (132 x 132 cm)

In late 1952, Cy Twombly, along with fellow artist Robert
Rauschenberg, traveled to Italy and North Africa on a fellowship.
Twombly arrived in Rome with a purpose, stating on his fellowship application that he was drawn "to the primitive, the ritual
and fetish elements, to the symmetrical plastic order." For
Twombly, this order mixed with ritual was made manifest in
ancient structures, in totemic stones and glyphic ruins, and these
forms enter into both his painting and his sculpture of the time.
Untitled is decidedly totemic, featuring a series of towers resem-
bling phalluses executed in quick washes of paint and frenetic
line work. In its essence, the work illustrates primal energy
transforming into architectural form, personal gestures building
and coalescing into archetypes. *Untitled* was made at the beginning of Twombly's career, but it is fundamental to understanding
the artist's lifelong passion for ancient societies and his belief in
the dynamism of art to revive their spirits and powers.

KARA WALKER

African't, 1996
Cut paper on wall
Overall 144 x 792 in. (365.7 x 2011 cm)

Kara Walker revives the 18th- and 19th-century art of silhouett-
ing, a long-dormant medium used for portraiture, caricatures,
idyllic landscapes, and decorative craft. Under Walker's hand and
scissors, the innocuous silhouette technique becomes a deadly
weapon, finding the shadows that lurk both in the annals of
history and in the silence of history's repressed voices. *African't*
receives its title from a derogatory slang term for pessimism in

the African American community. In the work, Walker's cutouts are nearly life size, spanning two walls of a room to become a theater of remembrance and forgetting. Here, blacks and whites, men, women, and children all participate in pre–Civil War scenes of degradation, sex, and violence. Walker summons archetypes, both clichéd and freshly shocking, to study how the real and imagined histories of trauma conspire to affect later generations.

JEFF WALL

Dead Troops Talk (a vision after an ambush of a Red Army patrol, near Moqor, Afghanistan, winter 1986), 1992
Transparency in lightbox
90 ⅛ x 164 ⅛ in. (228.9 x 416.8 cm)

One of the most influential photographers to emerge in the last 30 years, Jeff Wall creates elaborately staged transparencies that are displayed in light boxes. Wall's photographs conjure moments of strange resonance, mixing art historical references with subtle conceptual strategies and juxtapositions to offer a critique of modern living. In *Dead Troops Talk*, Wall captures an intricate

fictional scene that resembles at once a painting of war and a still from a zombie horror film. Staged in several parts, the photograph depicts a battlefield with soldiers coming back to life. The men show a range of emotional responses to their newfound transcendence, from humor to confusion. At the point where the troops could know the historical meaning of their own actions, they find themselves only concerned with interpersonal relationships.

ANDY WARHOL

Twenty Jackies, 1964
Silkscreen ink on linen
80 ½ x 80 ½ in. (204.4 x 204.4 cm)

On November 22, 1963, President John F. Kennedy was assassinated. In response to the tragic event, Andy Warhol began collecting large amounts of press coverage and photographs related to the assassination and its aftermath. For several years, Warhol had been drawn to images of the darker side of American life, documenting car crashes, race riots, and even the most wanted criminals on his silkscreened canvases. However, Warhol's *Twenty Jackies* focuses neither on the macabre details of the assassination nor on wide views of public mourning. Instead, using his powers as a portrait artist, Warhol finds the history of that dark November in the face of Jackie Kennedy, in the private counsel of an individual absorbed by loss. Warhol repeats the image of Jackie 20 times, mimicking the First Lady's high visibility in the media of the time. Yet, Warhol also allows the silkscreen and thus Jackie to fade with every printing. The more her image of grief is repeated, the less it is truly known.

CHRISTOPHER WOOL

Installation view of **Untitled**, 1990
Enamel and acrylic on nine aluminum panels
Each 96 x 64 in. (243.8 x 162.5 cm)

In the late 1980s, inspired by the graffiti of "sex" and "luv" on a white delivery truck, Christopher Wool began incorporating text into his work. The paintings that followed are perhaps Wool's most recognizable images. Applying black enamel through industrial-style letter stencils onto sheets of white-painted aluminum, Wool repurposes and reactivates passages from cultural idioms and song lyrics. *Untitled* features the words "Run" and "Dog" across a series of nine aluminum panels. The arrangement of the panels varies depending on where they are displayed,

thus meaning changes as the words are reordered. The resulting phrases are always frantic—sometimes composed as commands, "Run Dog Run," and other times as stuttered ramblings, "Dog Run Run." The words themselves are broken up within each panel, a small but thorny impediment to comprehension; they must be reassembled before being read. This delay makes the simple three-letter words—for a split second—unfamiliar.

PHOTOGRAPHY CREDITS